MEET MAX

Learning about Divorce from a Basset Hound's Perspective

Jennifer Leister, LPC

Illustrations by Raymond Reyes and Ramir Quintana

Dedication

For my loving family–Chris, Emma, and Rhett

4

My name is Max, and I'm a basset hound. I live with Sam, the best seven-year-old boy in the world.

Did you know that basset hounds were bred for hunting rabbits? I don't think Sam picked me to hunt rabbits with him, but he did pick me! Sam and I have been together every day since I was a little puppy.

Sam and I love playing. I make Sam laugh by chasing rabbits and playing catch with my favorite ball.

Sam likes watching me bury my toys in the backyard. Most of the time, I bury my toys. But sometimes, I find other interesting things to bury, like one of Sam's mommy's shoes. You should see Sam and me play!

Today I waited for Sam to come home from school so we could play. I found a new toy to bury, and I couldn't wait to show Sam!

But when Sam came home, his mom and dad yelled at each other with words that I didn't understand.

I don't think Sam understood them either.

Sam didn't feel like playing. He was very, very quiet instead. I think he was scared–and so was I.

That night it rained. When I heard thunder, I ran into Sam's room, just in case he was scared. His bed was warm and safe, and I spent the whole night under his blanket.

The next day, Sam's mommy and daddy weren't yelling anymore. They weren't talking to each other either.

The next night, Sam's dad slept on the couch instead of the bedroom. This made me really mad because the couch is my bed!

A few days later, Sam's daddy kissed Sam good-bye and said he was going to his new home. He said Sam will live in two homes.

"I don't want to live in your new home, Daddy," Sam cried. "I want you to stay here." Sam's daddy gave him a long hug. Sam's daddy was sad too.

Sam's daddy said it was time for him to go, and he left.

Sam was scared. So was I.

I didn't feel like playing outside anymore. I didn't want to play ball or bury shoes or toys.

And I didn't feel like chasing rabbits.

One morning after Sam's dad moved to his new home, my long-eared friend, Otis the Rabbit, hopped over to me. I always chased Otis, but not today.

"Why don't you chase me?" Otis asked.

"I don't want to play chase anymore," I said.

"Why, Max?" Otis asked. "Where's Sam?"

"Sam isn't here," I told him. "Sam is at his daddy's new home. It's Sam's new home too. His mommy and daddy got a divorce."

"What is a divorce?" Otis asked me.

"Divorce is when a mommy and daddy choose to not be married anymore. They choose to have two homes instead of one," I explained.

"Oh, so now Sam isn't always at your house, and that's why you're sad."

"Yes," I sniffed. "I'm glad Sam gets to spend time at his daddy's home, but I miss him when he's not here with me."

"Can Sam's parents divorce him?" Otis asked. "Who will take care of Sam?"

"No!" I replied. "Mommies and daddies can only divorce each other, not their kids. Sam's mommy and daddy love Sam very much, and they always will. They will be Sam's mommy and daddy forever. They just don't want to live together anymore."

"Well," Otis said, "sounds like Sam's mommy and daddy will still take care of him, so you don't need to worry! Now, do you want to play chase?"

"No, thanks. Not today."

The next day Otis hopped over to me. "Wanna play chase?" he asked again.

"No," I said. "I'm still sad."

"Do Sam's parents still love him? And does Sam still love you?" Otis asked.

"Yes, but Sam is still at his daddy's home. He isn't here to take me for a walk so we can play chase."

"But I'm here and I will play chase with you!" Otis said.

"No, thanks. Maybe I will feel like it tomorrow."

The next day, Otis came back again. "Want to play chase?"

"No. I still don't feel like it."

"Max, Sam loves you, and he doesn't want you to be sad when he's at his daddy's house."

I shook my head.

"Come on, Max! We'll play chase, and I'll even help you bury a pair of shoes!"

"I don't know, Otis, not today, not without Sam."

When Otis came back the next day, I couldn't wait to tell him the good news.

"Sam comes back to our house tonight. I can't wait to see him!"

"That's great!" Otis shouted. "Now, do you want to play chase?"

But I wasn't ready yet. "I'm waiting for Sam."

That night, Sam came back to our house. Sam told his mommy and me all about his great week.

"At first, I was worried. I didn't know if Daddy could help me with my homework. I didn't know how long it would take to get to school or baseball practice from Dad's new home. What if I was late?"

Sam's mommy smiled. "Your father knows how to help you with homework, Sam."

Sam nodded. "I know, Mommy—he did! And he drove me to school and practice on time. He packed my lunches and washed my baseball uniform too."

Sam pulled something out of his backpack. "Daddy even bought us a new ball to play catch with, Max!"

Boy, was I excited when I saw that ball! Then Sam said something that really made me wag my tail.

"And guess what else, Max? Daddy said some night, if it's okay with Mommy, you could have a sleepover with me at my other home. Does that sound like fun?"

You bet it did! That night, Sam and I played catch until bedtime. And I dug up an old pair of shoes–Sam brought them back to his mommy. She was glad to see them!

The next day, I showed Otis the new ball and told him everything Sam had said.

"I'm glad Sam's okay, Max."

"Me too. I think Sam was really worried at first, but staying at his daddy's house turned out to be just fine."

"Everybody worries when things change, Max," Otis said. "But now that you know Sam's happy, maybe you should be happy too."

"Maybe you're right, Otis." I scratched my nose. "You're pretty smart for a rabbit."

Otis grinned as he hopped away. "Smart enough to beat you in a game of chase!"

"You better run fast!" I shouted as I started to run after him. "Here I come!"

www.ingramcontent.com/pod-product-compliance
Lightning Source LLC
Chambersburg PA
CBHW042101040426
42448CB00002B/93